Wolfgang Amadeus
MOZART

SIX SONATAS

VOLUME I
(K. 10, 11, 12)

FOR FLUTE AND PIANO

K 03548

Kalmus

Sonata I
in Bb Major
K.V. 10

FLUTE

Wolfgang Amadeus Mozart
(1756-1791)

Menuetto primo

Menuetto secondo

Menuetto primo da capo

Sonata II
in G Major
K.V. 11

FLUTE

Wolfgang Amadeus Mozart
(1756-1791)

6

da capo Allegro

Sonata III
in A Major
K.V. 12

FLUTE

Wolfgang Amadeus Mozart
(1756-1791)

8

Wolfgang Amadeus
MOZART

8-00

SIX SONATAS

VOLUME I
(K. 10, 11, 12)

FOR FLUTE AND PIANO

K 03548

Sonata I
in Bb Major
K.V. 10

Wolfgang Amadeus Mozart
(1756-1791)

4

Menuetto primo

Menuetto secondo

Menuetto primo da Capo

Sonata II
in G Major
K.V. 11

Wolfgang Amadeus Mozart
(1756-1791)

14

16

Menuetto

Da Capo Allegro

Sonata III
in A Major
K.V. 12

Wolfgang Amadeus Mozart
(1756-1791)

20

22

Allegro

24